READY, SET, DRAW!

MANGA

AILIN CHAMBERS

 Gareth Stevens
PUBLISHING

Please visit our website, **www.garethstevens.com**. For a free color catalog of all our high-quality books, call toll free 1-800-542-2595 or fax 1-877-542-2596.

Library of Congress Cataloging-in-Publication Data

Chambers, Ailin.
Manga / by Ailin Chambers.
p. cm. — (Ready, set, draw!)
Includes index.
ISBN 978-1-4824-0919-2 (pbk.)
ISBN 978-1-4824-0920-8 (6-pack)
ISBN 978-1-4824-0918-5 (library binding)
1. Cartooning — Technique — Juvenile literature. 2. Comic books, strips, etc. — Japan — Technique — Juvenile literature. 3. Comic strip characters — Juvenile literature. I. Chambers, Ailin. II. Title.
NC1764.5.J3 C43 2015
741.5—d23

First Edition

Published in 2015 by
Gareth Stevens Publishing
111 East 14th Street, Suite 349
New York, NY 10003

Copyright © Arcturus Holdings Limited

Editors: Samantha Hilton, Kate Overy and Joe Harris
Illustrations: Dynamo Limited
Design concept: Keith Williams
Design: Dynamo Limited and Notion Design
Cover design: Ian Winton

Printed in the United States of America

CPSIA compliance information: Batch #CS15GS: For further information contact Gareth Stevens, New York, New York at 1-800-542-2595.

CONTENTS

GRAB THESE!

Are you ready to create some amazing pictures? Wait a minute! Before you begin drawing, you will need a few important pieces of equipment.

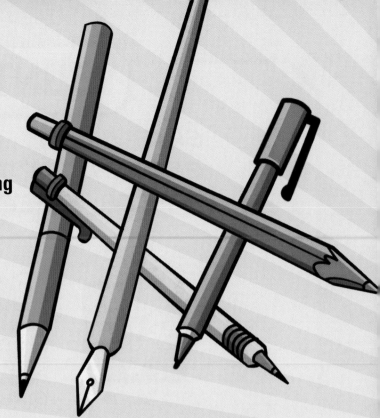

PENCILS

You can use a variety of drawing tools, such as pens, chalks, pencils, and paints. But to begin use an ordinary pencil.

PAPER

Use a clean sheet of paper for your final drawings. Scrap paper is useful and cheap for your practice work.

ERASERS

Everyone makes mistakes! That's why every artist has a good eraser. When you erase a mistake, do it gently. Erasing too hard will ruin your drawing and possibly even rip it.

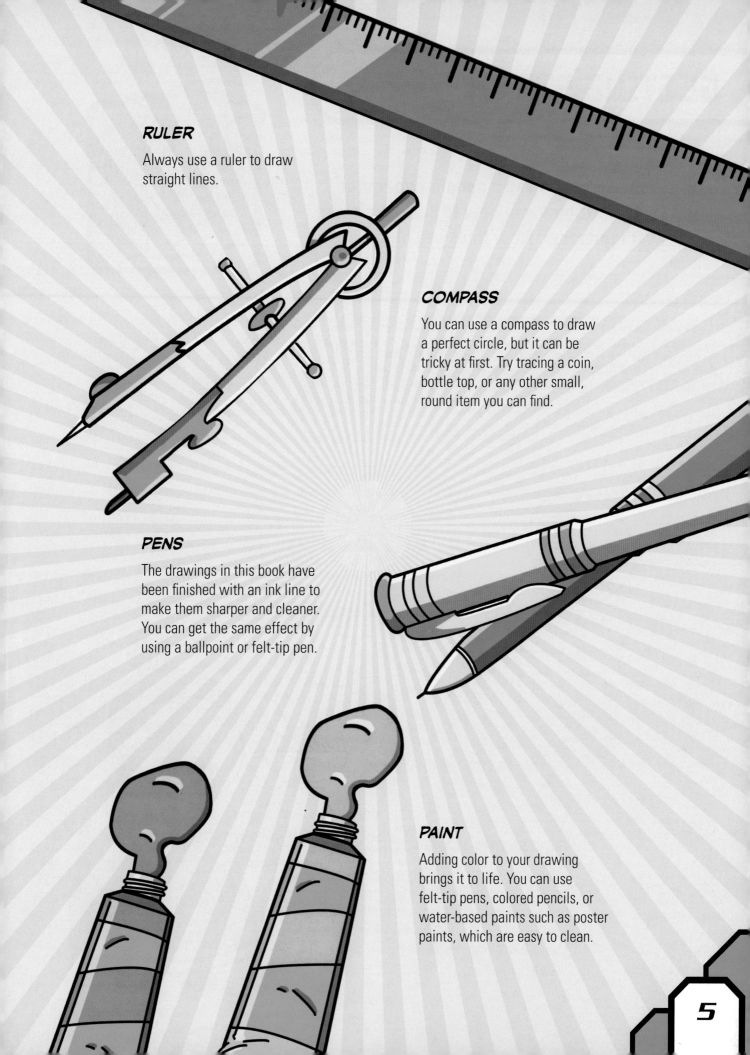

RULER

Always use a ruler to draw straight lines.

COMPASS

You can use a compass to draw a perfect circle, but it can be tricky at first. Try tracing a coin, bottle top, or any other small, round item you can find.

PENS

The drawings in this book have been finished with an ink line to make them sharper and cleaner. You can get the same effect by using a ballpoint or felt-tip pen.

PAINT

Adding color to your drawing brings it to life. You can use felt-tip pens, colored pencils, or water-based paints such as poster paints, which are easy to clean.

GETTING STARTED

In this book we use a simple two—color system to show you how to draw a picture. Just remember: New lines are blue lines!

STARTING WITH STEP 1

The first lines you will draw are very simple shapes. They will be shown in blue. You should draw them with a normal pencil.

ADDING MORE DETAIL

As you move on to the next step, the lines you have already drawn will be shown in black. The new lines for that step will appear in blue.

FINISHING YOUR PICTURE

When you reach the final stage, you will see the image in full color with a black ink line. Inking a picture means tracing the main lines with a black pen. After the ink dries, use your eraser to remove all the pencil lines before adding your color.

SPECIAL EFFECTS

You can make your drawings more exciting by adding special effects. It will also make your stories more fun if your characters have special powers. Here are some basic effects you can use on your creations:

LIGHTNING BLAST

Give your characters lightning powers! Add blue, jagged lines coming from their hands or weapons. This will make it look like they are shooting lightning bolts.

MAGIC STARS

Why not give some characters magical powers? Add different-sized stars around their hands.

HEATING IT UP

Give your characters fire powers by adding flames. Flames are rounded at the bottom but shaped like wavy spikes at the top. Color the center of the flames in a light yellow.

VILLAIN

There's no doubt that this guy is a villain.
His pale, sneering face and red, robotic eye
make him look really scary!

STEP 1

Start by drawing the shape
of your villain's long body
and legs. Add a head with a
pointy chin.

STEP 2

Then, draw two straight
lines to make his legs
and waist.

STEP 3

Next, draw his arms and feet.
Add two ears and two lines
for his nose. Join the head to
the body with a neck. Draw
two short lines for the collar
of his jacket.

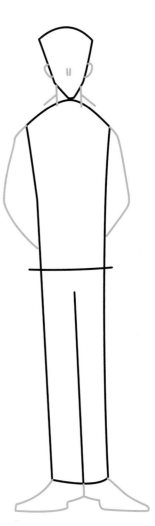

STEP 6

Color him using shades such as purple, red, black and blue. Use shading around the edges.

STEP 4

Add long, curved lines to make the shape and folds of his suit. Don't forget his hairline and his scary, robotic eye.

STEP 5

Now you can add his shirt, tie, and crazy hair. Add the rest of his robotic eye and a small mouth. Finally, finish his pants.

SUPER TIP!

You can make your villain look even more frightening by giving him incredible mind powers.

- Draw a jagged semicircle around his head. Then, add long, wavy lines that spread outward.

GIRL GENIUS

With her big glasses and white lab coat, Girl Genius looks super brainy. She's always thinking up new inventions to save the world from danger.

STEP 1

First, draw her white lab coat and her head.

STEP 2

Next, draw two sausage-like shapes for the tops of her arms.

STEP 3

Add forearms, wide pants and the outline of her hair.

STEP 4

Draw her face and neck. Add hands, feet, and the opening of her lab coat.

STEP 5

Add her glasses, the details on her face and coat, and her flasks.

STEP 6

Finally, color her in. Leave her jacket white so that it looks like a scientist's lab coat.

FIRE SPIRIT

The Fire Spirit is an evil creature with magical powers. He has a long face, pointy ears, and a nasty grin. He wants to set the whole world on fire!

STEP 1

First, draw a tall shape like this for the spirit's robe.

STEP 2

Add his pointy head and the wide sleeves of his robe.

STEP 3

Draw his long, pointy ears, his neck, his claw-like fingers, and the flames around his feet.

STEP 4

Now, draw the flames shooting out of his hands and around his feet. The flames should curl upwards.

STEP 5

Draw his evil eyes, tiny nose, and sneaky smile. Give his eyes tiny black pupils to make him look really wicked. Then, add lines for the folds in his long, flowing robe.

STEP 6

Color your villain in shades of purple, red, and yellow.

SUPER TIP!

- When colring in flames, start with a yellow color in the middle part of the flames.

- Add red and orange colors as you move toward the outside of your flames.

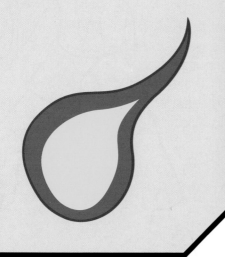

ANCIENT WARRIOR

This warrior is armed only with a simple wooden staff. His face is hidden beneath a wide-brimmed straw hat.

STEP 1

First, draw the warrior's bean-shaped body and the lower part of his jacket. Don't forget the wide fan shape for his hat.

STEP 2

Add his curved legs.

STEP 3

Next, draw his chin, feet, and wide sleeves.

STEP 4

Sketch his hair, beard, nose, and mouth. Draw his hands, and curve his fingers as if they're gripping something. Draw lines to make the tops of his slippers and his belt.

STEP 5

Draw a staff in his clenched hands, and add detail to his wide hat.

STEP 6

Color your ancient warrior. Shade his face and shoulder to show the shadow cast by his hat.

MARTIAL ARTIST

This martial artist is crouching low to the ground, ready to attack. His special pose and determined face tell us he's a skilled fighter.

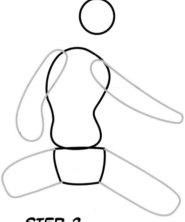

STEP 1

First, draw a peanut shape for his body and a pot shape for his hips. Add a small circle for his head.

STEP 2

Add sausage-like shapes for his arms and thighs.

STEP 3

Draw his pointed chin, hands, and lower legs.

STEP 4

Carefully draw his feet, cuffs, and hair.

STEP 5

Add his narrow eyes, nose, and serious mouth. Then, draw the final details of his clothing.

SUPER TIP!

The strapping on this martial artist's leg is easy to draw. Just follow these steps:

- First, draw your straps as simple crossing lines down his leg.

- Add lines on either side.

- Erase the lines you started with and color in the straps.

STEP 6

Color your martial artist. Use shading to make him stand out from the page.

MINI MONSTER

This big-eyed mini monster looks cute. He has huge ears and long whiskers. Does he fight other mini monsters in an arena, or is he a pet? You decide!

STEP 1

First, draw a shape like a peanut.

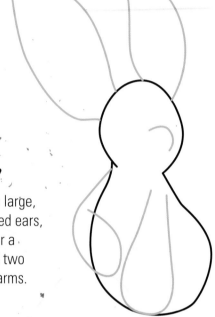

STEP 2

Draw two large, leaf-shaped ears, a curve for a nose, and two club-like arms.

STEP 3

Add a long, curved tail, back legs, and a pointy forehead.

STEP 4

Now, draw his big eyes, small mouth, and claws. Sketch details for the left ear and the back paws.

STEP 5

Add long whiskers. Then, cover your mini monster's body in spots, or stripes if you prefer.

STEP 6

Now, color your mini monster in any shade you like. When it comes to monsters, there are no rules. Anything goes!

MAGICAL GIRL

This fun-loving magical girl looks like she's about to leap off the page. She has big, cute eyes and bright blue hair!

STEP 1

Start by drawing the girl's body and head.

STEP 2

Add sausage-shaped upper arms and a wide skirt.

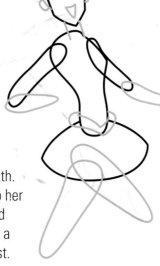

STEP 3

Draw ears and a mouth. Now, join her head to her body with a neck. Add forearms, thighs, and a band around her waist.

STEP 4

Add her hair, hands, and lower legs. Don't forget her collar and the bow that's behind her waist.

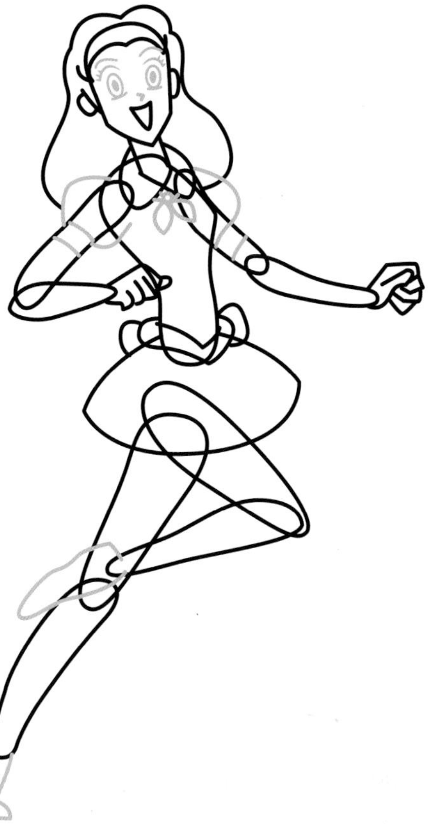

STEP 5

Sketch her sleeves, tie, and feet before adding her eyes.

STEP 6

Finally, you're ready to add some color. Bright and bold colors look best.

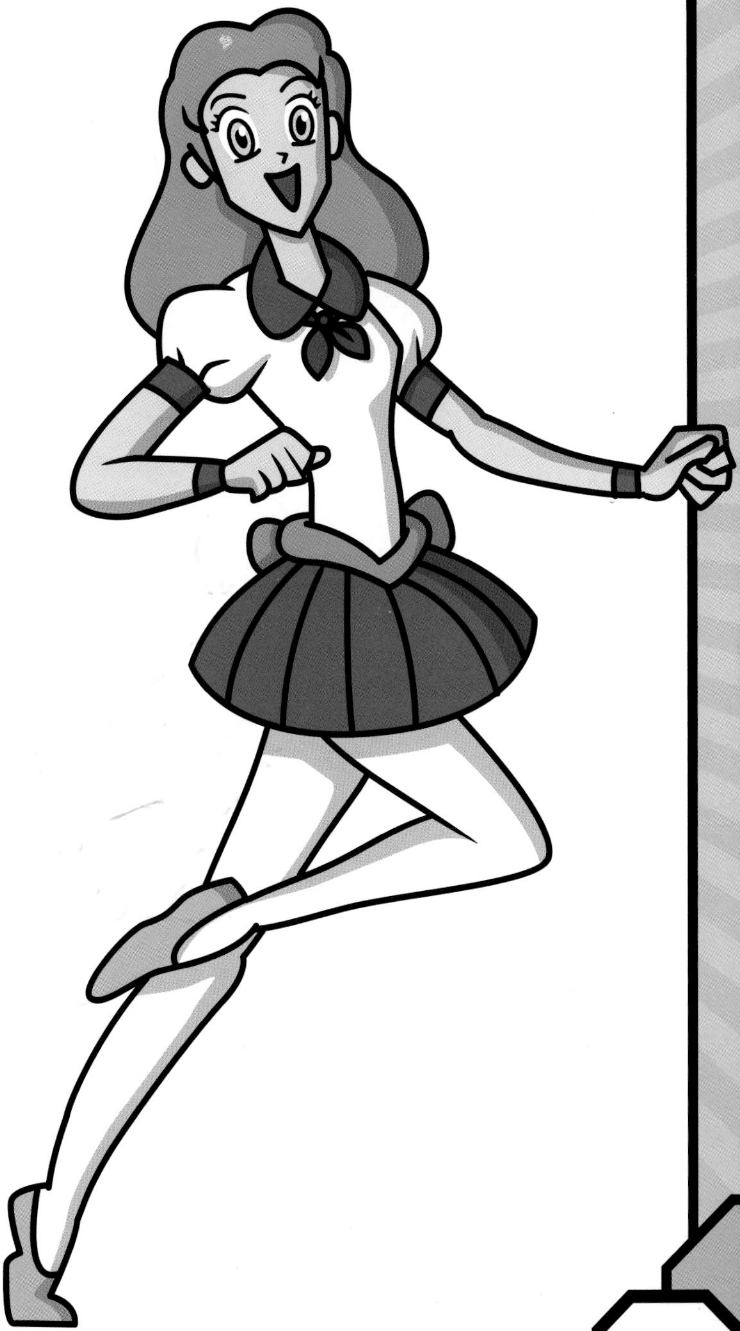

SUPER TIP!

Manga eyes are easy to draw if you build them up from simple, round shapes.

- Draw two ovals for the main outlines of the eyes.
- Add large irises in the center.
- Use two curves to make the tops of the eyes. Add lines at the bottom for the lower eyelids.
- Draw a couple of eyebrows, and you have your big manga eyes!

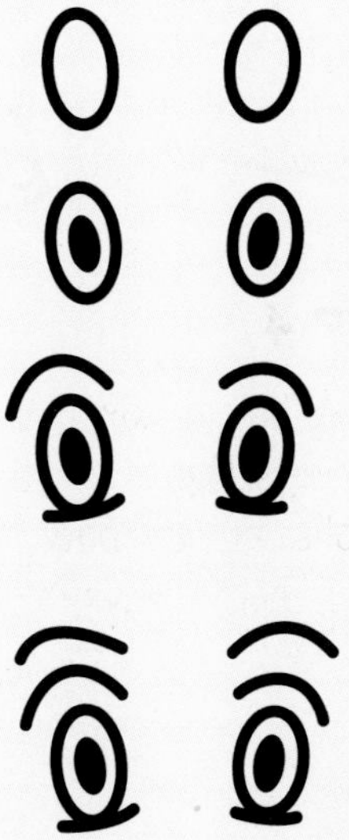

SAMURAI

Samurai were brave Japanese warriors. This one is tall and proud with a square jaw. He wears a green robe and carries a long samurai sword.

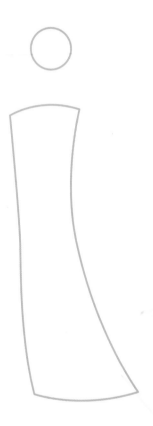

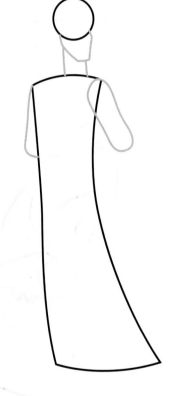

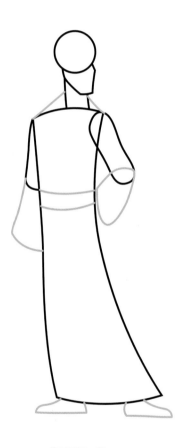

STEP 1

First, draw a long, curved rectangle for the samurai's robe. Add a small circle for his head.

STEP 2

Draw a square jaw and two lines for his neck. Then, draw sausage-shaped arms.

STEP 3

Next, add his shoulders and the sleeves of his robe. Draw his belt and feet.

STEP 4

Draw his hairline, hands, and wooden clogs. Add the edging to his robe.

STEP 6

Finally, color your samurai. A strong green color makes his robe stand out.

STEP 5

Draw his face, long sword, and topknot. Add detalis to the wooden clogs.

LITTLE OLD LADY

This lady is very happy. Her round body makes her look very cuddly and kind. Her open mouth and closed eyes show that she's laughing.

STEP 1

Draw a mushroom shape for her upper body and a pebble shape for her head.

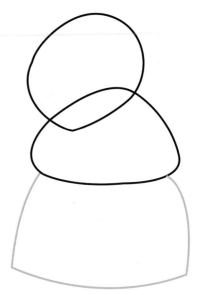

STEP 2

Draw a thick shape for her lower body.

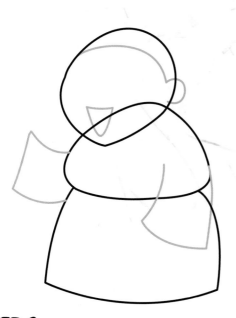

STEP 3

Add her hairline and mouth. Then, draw the wide sleeves of her robe.

STEP 4

Carefully draw her hands, hair, nose, and belt.

STEP 5

Add the final details, including curves for her eyes and her bowl of noodles.

STEP 6

Color the little old lady in soft colors.

CAT GIRL

This girl has a cat's furry tail, big ears and long whiskers. She loves playing tricks on people!

STEP 1

First, draw an oval for her head and this curved shape for her body.

STEP 2

Draw two sausage-like shapes for her legs, and draw her long arms.

STEP 3

Add her cat-like ears and the rest of her legs.

STEP 4

Her curved tail comes next. Then, add her neck, the details of her clothing, her hands, her feet and her face. Don't forget those big eyes!

STEP 5

Draw her shaggy hair wrapping around the front of her ears. Add details to her cuff and shoes.

STEP 6

You could add streaks to her hair or leave it bright pink like this. Her whiskers are the finishing touch!

Sumo wrestlers are very large. This one squats down low as he faces his opponent. During fights, a sumo wears a silk loincloth called a mawashi.

STEP 1

Sumos are large, so start the body and head with these big, round shapes.

STEP 2

Add his rounded arms and legs, as well as his mawashi.

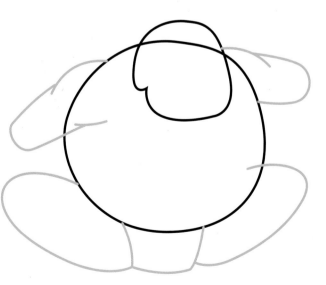

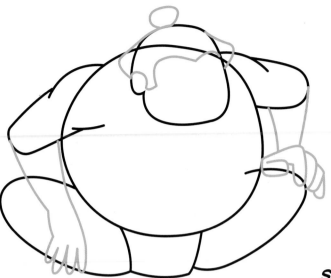

STEP 3

Add the rest of his arms and hands.
Then, draw the sumo's hairstyle.

STEP 4

Add details to his
chest. Finish his
legs and feet.

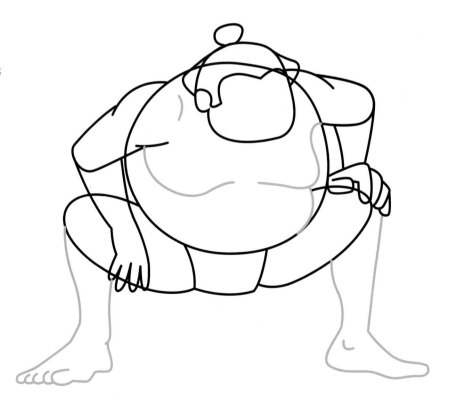

STEP 5

Draw his face and hair. He has heavy eyebrows, a wide mouth, and a fierce expression. Add the pieces hanging down from his mawashi. They are called sagari.

STEP 6

Sumo wrestlers believe the color of their mawashi affects their luck in matches. Red must be this sumo's lucky color!

GLOSSARY

arena An enclosed area, often circular or oval-shaped, for performances.

clog A wooden shoe.

cuff The end of a sleeve, around the wrist.

iris The coloured central part of the eye.

loincloth A piece of cloth that wraps around the hips.

pupil In an eye, the black circle in the center of the iris, which controls the amount of light entering the eye.

staff A long stick used as a support for walking or as a weapon.

FURTHER READING

How to Draw Manga by David Antram (Book House, 2010)

Kids Draw Big Book of Everything Manga by Chris Hart (Watson-Guptill Publications Inc., 2009)

WEBSITES

www.drawingnow.com/how-to-draw-manga.html

www.howtodrawmanga.com

www.wikihow.com/Draw-Manga

INDEX